T0337311

THE LITTLE BOOK OF

NEGRONI

HarperCollins*Publishers*
1 London Bridge Street
London SE1 9GF

www.harpercollins.co.uk

HarperCollins*Publishers*
Macken House, 39/40 Mayor Street Upper
Dublin 1, D01 C9W8, Ireland

First published by HarperCollins*Publishers* 2024

13 5 7 9 10 8 6 4 2

A catalogue record of this book is available from the British Library

ISBN 978-0-00-871338-6

Printed and bound in Latvia

MIX
Paper | Supporting
responsible forestry
FSC™ C007454

This book is produced from independently certified FSC™ paper to ensure responsible forest management.

For more information visit: www.harpercollins.co.uk/green

DISCLAIMER: The publisher urges readers to drink responsibly.

This book features recipes that include the optional use of raw eggs. Consuming raw eggs may increase the risk of food-borne illness. Individuals who are immunocompromised, pregnant or elderly should use caution. Ensure eggs are fresh and meet local food-standard requirements.

THE LITTLE BOOK OF

NEGRONI

PAUL KNORR

HarperCollins*Publishers*

CONTENTS

INTRODUCTION

The Negroni is the perfect cocktail. Simple to make but complex in flavour and open to endless variations. A combination of gin, Campari and sweet vermouth in equal parts. Any one (or more!) of those ingredients can be swapped out for something else, changing the drink completely but still preserving that complexity.

A drink that is less sweet and complex in flavour is what today's discerning drinkers are looking for, and a Negroni fits that bill perfectly. Invented in 1919 (or perhaps in 1865), the Negroni is not a new drink. It takes us back to an earlier time when cocktails were all the rage. Even so, it languished for many years, rarely seen outside of Italy. Now is its time to shine.

HISTORY OF THE NEGRONI

The history of the Negroni is, to put it mildly, complicated. There are two different origin stories for the drink, one placing it in Florence, Italy, in 1919 and the other in Senegal in 1865. While the Italian version of the story has been oft-repeated in magazines and websites, neither has any hard evidence to back it up. Printed versions of the drink don't begin to appear in cocktail collections until 1950.

The Italian version of the story is the more commonly accepted of the two and it starts with a similar drink called the Milano-Torino. The Milano-Torino is a combination of Campari, which is made in Milan, and Cinzano Sweet Vermouth, which hails from Turin. Soda water is then added at the end. Some may recognize this as a drink called the Americano. Allegedly, in 1919, a Count Camillo Negroni requested from bartender Fosco Scarselli, at the Caffe Casoni in Florence, a stronger version of the Milano-Torino that replaced the soda water with gin. The drink was a hit and Sr. Scarselli named the drink in the Count's honour.

The version from Senegal is based on an account by Noel Negroni, a verified descendant of General Pascal Olivier de Negroni de Cardi of Corsica. There is far more documentation about Pascal Negroni than there is of Count Camillo Negroni, including his participation in several important battles of the Franco-Prussian War. Between 1855 and 1865, he was the commander of a base in Saint Louis, Senegal. While there he wrote in a letter to his older brother Roche: 'Incidentally, did you know that the vermouth-based cocktail that I invented in Saint Louis is a great hit at the Lunéville Officers Club?' The letter was discovered by Noel Negroni and preserved as evidence of his ancestor's hand in the creation of this most wonderful cocktail.

Which story is the truth is difficult to discern and there has been much debate in the Negroni community over it. Ultimately it has no bearing on the enjoyment of a perfect cocktail.

ABOUT CAMPARI

Campari is an Italian bitter liqueur that is 48 proof (24% ABV). It is part of the 'amaro' family of Italian bitter herbal liqueurs, along with the likes of Cynar and Amaro Averna. Campari was invented by Gaspare Campari in Novara, Italy, in 1860. It is made from an infusion of herbs and fruit in alcohol and water. Up until 2006, Campari's distinctive bright red colour came from carmine dye, which is made from crushed cochineal insects. What it uses now is a trade secret.

Campari is currently produced by the Davide Campari Group (named after Gaspare's son) and is sold throughout the world.

'The bitters are excellent for your liver, the gin is bad for you. They balance each other.'

– Orson Welles

ABOUT GIN

Gin is a distilled alcoholic liquor that is typically 80 proof (40% ABV). The one constant flavour in gin is juniper berries, from which the word 'gin' comes. Additional flavours that are added can vary widely and produce an extensive variety of styles of gin. The style of gin typically used in a Negroni is called 'London Dry', which is first distilled from grain as a neutral spirit, then distilled a second time with juniper berries and other flavourings.

ABOUT SWEET VERMOUTH

Vermouth is a fortified and flavoured wine that comes in two varieties: sweet and dry. Vermouth is created by distilling a spirit from grain along with a proprietary blend of herbs, berries and roots that varies by producer. The aromatic spirit is then added to the base wine. Both sweet and dry vermouths have additional sugar, but sweet vermouth has a bit more than the dry.

The addition of alcohol and herbs to wine was first documented in China between 1250 and 1000 BC. The vermouth that we know today originates from Turin, Italy, in the 1850s. For a Negroni, using a good-quality vermouth is key. It is strongly recommended to use a vermouth from Turin, which has 'Torino' on the label.

GLASSWARE

Rocks glass – also known as an
old-fashioned, this traditional
tumbler is meant for a small
or strong drinks served over
ice. Most famously used for a

straight whisky 'on the rocks', the glass has a flat
base, a wide mouth for appreciating your drink's
aroma and is usually made from thickened glass
to stop the rocks melting.

Collins glass – about twice as tall
as a rocks glass, with a flat base
and straight sides, this is a glass
for long cocktails served over
ice and topped up with soda,
such as the Tom Collins it is
named after. The glass is also
tall enough to accommodate

garnishes dropped into a drink, such as slices of
citrus fruit and cherries.

Martini glass – with its V-shaped cup and a long stem, the classic cocktail glass is used for smaller or stronger drinks that are served 'up', meaning without any ice in them. The most obvious  example of a drink served in a martini glass would of course be a martini, but it suits any cocktail with a garnish because of its wide rim.

Coupe glass – similar to a martini glass but with a rounded, bowl-shaped cup and usually a shorter stem for extra stability. The coupe is popular for frozen drinks because the stem keeps the drinker's hot hand away from cocktails that have been shaken over or blended with ice. Originally designed to show off the bubbles and aroma of Champagne, a coupe also suits a cocktail requiring a creative garnish on the rim.

DRINKS RECIPES

The drinks writer Brad Thomas Parsons asks the question: 'What is the tipping point when a Negroni is no longer a Negroni?' Perhaps this collection of variations, both close and very far from the original, will help to determine that point.

TRADITIONAL NEGRONI

INGREDIENTS

30 ml (1 fl oz) London Dry Gin

30 ml (1 fl oz) Campari

30 ml (1 fl oz) sweet vermouth (preferably
one from Turin, Italy)

Orange wheel, to garnish

METHOD

Add all the ingredients, except the garnish, to a
mixing glass half-filled with ice. Stir and strain
into a rocks glass over fresh ice. Garnish with an
orange wheel.

DIFFICULTY ★★

ACHTUNG: NEGRONI

INGREDIENTS

30 ml (1 fl oz) gin

30 ml (1 fl oz) Jägermeister

30 ml (1 fl oz) sweet vermouth

METHOD

Add all the ingredients to a rocks glass filled with ice and stir.

DIFFICULTY ★

'My Dear Negroni:
You say you can
drink, smoke,
and I am sure laugh,
just as much as ever.
I feel you are not
much to be pitied:
You must not take
more than
20 Negronis in
one day.'

– Francis Harper (friend of Count
Camillo Negroni), 1920

ALFREDO

INGREDIENTS

45 ml (1 ½ fl oz) gin
45 ml (1 ½ fl oz) Campari
Orange wheel, to garnish

METHOD

Add ice to a cocktail shaker, then add the gin and
Campari. Stir and strain into a rocks glass over
fresh ice. Twist an orange wheel before adding it
to the glass.

DIFFICULTY ★★

FUN FACT

A Negroni with Gordon's Dry Gin was the drink of choice for James Bond in Ian Fleming's short story, *Risico* (1960).

AMERICANO (THE 'PRE-NEGRONI')

INGREDIENTS

45 ml (1½ fl oz) Campari

45 ml (1½ fl oz) sweet vermouth

Club soda

Orange wheel, to garnish

METHOD

Add the Campari and sweet vermouth to a Collins glass filled with ice and stir. Top up with club soda and garnish with an orange wheel.

DIFFICULTY ★

ANNIVERSARY COCKTAIL

INGREDIENTS

60 ml (2 fl oz) gin

30 ml (1 fl oz) Cynar

30 ml (1 fl oz) Galliano

7 ml (¼ fl oz) orange juice

METHOD

Add all the ingredients to a cocktail shaker half-filled with ice and shake. Strain into a martini glass.

DIFFICULTY ★★

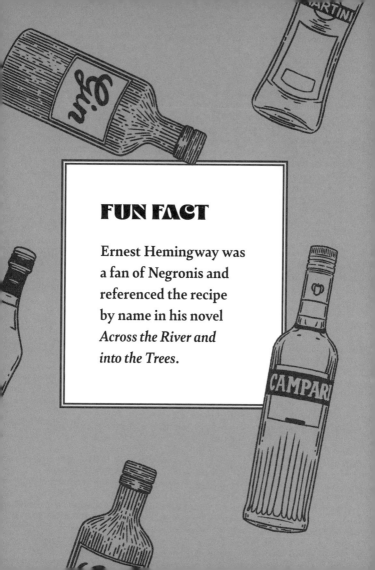

FUN FACT

Ernest Hemingway was a fan of Negronis and referenced the recipe by name in his novel *Across the River and into the Trees*.

BLACKBERRY NEGRONI

INGREDIENTS

30 ml (1 fl oz) gin
30 ml (1 fl oz) Campari
30 ml (1 fl oz) Chambord
Orange wedge, to garnish
Blackberry, to garnish

METHOD

Build over ice in a cocktail shaker and stir. Strain into a rocks glass over fresh ice. Garnish with an orange wedge and a blackberry.

DIFFICULTY ★★

'And now the sun is in your stomach.'

– Stanley Tucci,
Taste: My Life Through Food

THE BOULEVARDIER

INGREDIENTS

30 ml (1 fl oz) bourbon

30 ml (1 fl oz) Campari

30 ml (1 fl oz) sweet vermouth

Orange twist, to garnish

METHOD

Build over ice in a rocks glass and stir. Garnish with an orange twist.

DIFFICULTY ★

From Barflies and Cocktails
by Harry McElhone, 1927

BRENTON NEGRONI

INGREDIENTS

40 ml (1 ¼ fl oz) Malfy Italian Gin

20 ml (¾ fl oz) La Pivón Vermouth Blanco

20 ml (¾ fl oz) Luxardo Bitter Bianco

7 ml (¼ fl oz) grapefruit juice

3 dashes of rhubarb bitters

METHOD

Add all the ingredients to a cocktail shaker half-filled with ice and shake. Strain over fresh ice into a rocks glass.

DIFFICULTY ★★

From Maurice Taylor, Bartending Supervisor, Brenton Hotel, Newport, Rhode Island, USA

CAMPANILE

INGREDIENTS

30 ml (1 fl oz) gin

15 ml (½ fl oz) Campari

15 ml (½ fl oz) apricot brandy

7 ml (¼ fl oz) orange juice

METHOD

Add all the ingredients to a cocktail shaker half-filled with ice and shake. Strain into a martini glass.

DIFFICULTY ★★

THE CARDINALE

INGREDIENTS

30 ml (1 fl oz) gin
30 ml (1 fl oz) Campari
30 ml (1 fl oz) dry vermouth
Orange wheel, to garnish

METHOD

Add all the ingredients, except the garnish, to a
cocktail shaker half-filled with ice and stir. Strain
into a rocks glass filled with fresh ice. Garnish with
an orange wheel.

DIFFICULTY ★★

From the Hotel Excelsior, Rome,
Italy, in the 1950s

CHERRY NEGRONI

INGREDIENTS

30 ml (1 fl oz) gin
20 ml (¾ fl oz) Campari
20 ml (¾ fl oz) sweet vermouth
15 ml (½ fl oz) amaretto
7 ml (¼ fl oz) maraschino cherry juice
Maraschino cherry, to garnish

METHOD

Add all the ingredients, except the garnish, to a cocktail shaker half-filled with ice and stir. Strain into a rocks glass filled with fresh ice. Garnish with a maraschino cherry.

DIFFICULTY ★★

'If somebody orders a Negroni, you think "okay, you're cool."'

– Paul Mescal

COSMOGRONI

INGREDIENTS

30 ml (1 fl oz) citrus vodka
30 ml (1 fl oz) vermouth bianco
15 ml (½ fl oz) Aperol
15 ml (½ fl oz) Cointreau
Dash of cranberry bitters
Orange wheel, to garnish

METHOD

Add all the ingredients, except the garnish, to
a cocktail shaker half-filled with ice and stir.
Strain into a martini glass and garnish with an
orange wheel.

DIFFICULTY ★★

*Adapted from a recipe by J.P. Fetherston
and Alex Levy, Columbia Room,
Washington, DC, USA*

DEAR JANE

INGREDIENTS

30 ml (1 fl oz) gin

30 ml (1 fl oz) Campari

20 ml (¾ fl oz) sweet vermouth

7 ml (¼ fl oz) elderflower liqueur

Lemon twist, to garnish

METHOD

Add all the ingredients, except the garnish, to a rocks glass. Fill with ice and stir. Garnish with a lemon twist.

DIFFICULTY ★

*Created by Zachary Gelnaw-Rubin
at Attaboy, NYC, USA, in 2015*

FROZEN NEGRONI

Makes 6 drinks

INGREDIENTS

125 ml (4 fl oz) gin
125 ml (4 fl oz) sweet vermouth
125 ml (4 fl oz) Campari
350 ml (12 fl oz) orange juice
1 kg (4 cups) ice
6 orange wheels, to garnish

METHOD

Add all the ingredients, except the garnish, to a blender and blend until smooth. Pour into 6 rock glasses and garnish each with an orange wheel.

DIFFICULTY ★★

THE GLORIA

INGREDIENTS

45 ml (1½ fl oz) gin
15 ml (½ fl oz) Campari
15 ml (½ fl oz) dry vermouth
15 ml (½ fl oz) Cointreau
Lemon twist, to garnish

METHOD

In a cocktail shaker half-filled with ice, add all the ingredients, except the garnish, and stir. Strain into a martini glass and garnish with a lemon twist.

DIFFICULTY ★★

Created by French silent movie star Marie Glory as part of a cocktail competition in 1929, according to the Cointreau website. Other sources attribute the drink to Trader Vic around 1947, as it appears in one of his bartending manuals.

ITALIAN STALLION

INGREDIENTS

45 ml (1½ fl oz) bourbon
20 ml (¾ fl oz) Campari
20 ml (¾ fl oz) sweet vermouth
Orange twist, to garnish

METHOD

In a cocktail shaker half-filled with ice, add all
the ingredients, except the garnish, and stir. Strain
into a rocks glass over fresh ice. Garnish with an
orange twist.

DIFFICULTY ★★

JASMINE

INGREDIENTS

45 ml (1 ½ fl oz) gin
15 ml (½ fl oz) Cointreau
15 ml (½ fl oz) Campari
30 ml (1 fl oz) lemon juice
Lemon twist, to garnish

METHOD

In a cocktail shaker half-filled with ice, add all
the ingredients, except the garnish, and stir. Strain
into a rocks glass over fresh ice. Garnish with a
lemon twist.

DIFFICULTY ★★

'The good lion would sit and fold his wings back and ask politely if he might have a Negroni or an Americano and he always drank that instead of the blood of the Hindu traders.'

– *The Good Lion* by Ernest Hemingway

MARTINI MILANO

INGREDIENTS

30 ml (1 fl oz) gin

15 ml (½ fl oz) Campari

15 ml (½ fl oz) dry vermouth

White wine

Lemon twist, to garnish

METHOD

In a cocktail shaker half-filled with ice, add all the ingredients except for the white wine and lemon and stir. Strain into a Collins glass filled with fresh ice and top up with the white wine. Garnish with a lemon twist.

DIFFICULTY ★★

MEZCAL NEGRONI

INGREDIENTS

30 ml (1 fl oz) mezcal

30 ml (1 fl oz) Campari

30 ml (1 fl oz) sweet vermouth

Orange twist, to garnish

METHOD

In a cocktail shaker half-filled with ice, add all the ingredients, except the garnish, and stir. Strain into a rocks glass over fresh ice. Garnish with an orange twist.

DIFFICULTY ★★

'A Negroni is a perfect drink as far as I'm concerned.'

– Anthony Bourdain

FUN FACT

The most expensive Negroni is the version from Maybe Sammy in Sydney, Australia. It consists of Gordon's Dry Gin from the 1970s, Campari from the 1970s and Carpano Vermouth from the 1960s. The price is AU$150.

NAPOLI

INGREDIENTS

30 ml (1 fl oz) gin
30 ml (1 fl oz) Campari
15 ml (½ fl oz) sweet vermouth
15 ml (½ fl oz) dry vermouth
Club soda
Orange wheel, to garnish

METHOD

Add all the ingredients except for the club soda and orange to a rocks glass filled with ice. Stir and top up with club soda. Garnish with an orange wheel.

DIFFICULTY ★

NEGRONI ABSINTHE

INGREDIENTS

7 ml (¼ fl oz) absinthe
45 ml (1 ½ fl oz) mezcal
20 ml (¾ fl oz) sweet vermouth
20 ml (¾ fl oz) Campari
7 ml (¼ fl oz) crème de cacao
Black liquorice stick, to garnish
Lemon twist, to garnish

METHOD

Coat the inside of a rocks glass with the absinthe
and dump out any excess. In a mixing glass with
ice, stir the remaining ingredients except the
garnishes, then strain into the coated glass. Garnish
with a black liquorice stick and a lemon twist.

DIFFICULTY ★★

NEGRONI EXTRA

INGREDIENTS

60ml (2 fl oz) gin

30ml (1 fl oz) Campari

30ml (1 fl oz) sweet vermouth

METHOD

Add all the ingredients to a shaker half-filled with ice. Shake and strain into a coupe glass.

DIFFICULTY ★★

NEGRONI SBAGLIATO ('WRONG' NEGRONI)

INGREDIENTS

30 ml (1 fl oz) prosecco

30 ml (1 fl oz) Campari

30 ml (1 fl oz) sweet vermouth

METHOD

Build over ice in a rocks glass and stir.

DIFFICULTY ★

*Allegedly created by accident in 1972 by
bartender Mirko Stocchetto of Bar Basso,
in Milan, when he picked up a bottle of
sparkling wine instead of gin.*

'It will hit you like a freight train after four or five.'

– Anthony Bourdain

NEGRONI SOUR

INGREDIENTS

30 ml (1 fl oz) gin
30 ml (1 fl oz) Campari
30 ml (1 fl oz) sweet vermouth
15 ml (½ fl oz) orange juice
15 ml (½ fl oz) lemon juice
1 small egg white*

*The egg white is meant to give the drink a foamy top. Aquafaba or Fee Foam by Fee Brothers can be substituted.

METHOD

Add all the ingredients to a cocktail shaker half-filled with ice. Shake vigorously and strain into a coupe glass.

DIFFICULTY ★★★

NEGRONI SWIZZLE

INGREDIENTS

30 ml (1 fl oz) gin
30 ml (1 fl oz) Campari
30 ml (1 fl oz) sweet vermouth
Club soda
Orange wheel or twist, to garnish

METHOD

Add all the ingredients except the club soda and garnish to a Collins glass filled with ice and stir. Top up with club soda and garnish with an orange wheel or orange twist.

DIFFICULTY ★

'It is said that Negronis are like breasts: "One is not enough, two is perfect, and three is just too many." Today I am tempted to see what happens if I drink four.'

– Stanley Tucci,
Taste: My Life Through Food

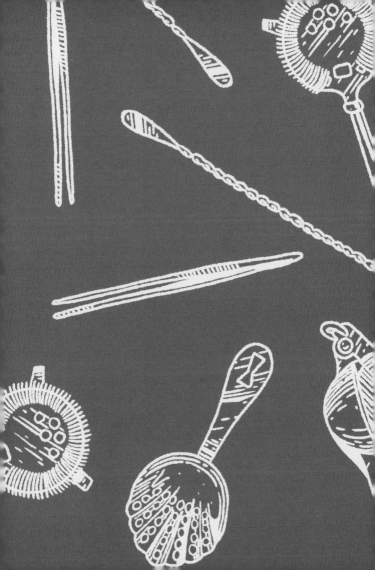

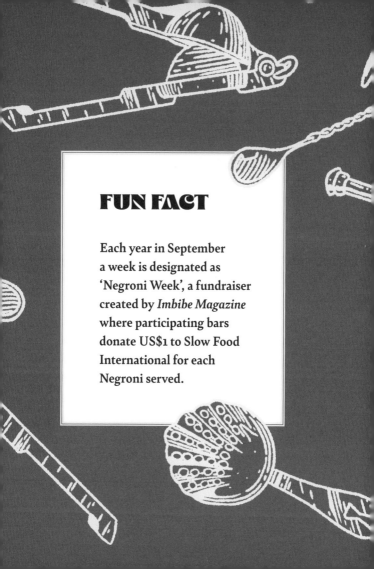

FUN FACT

Each year in September
a week is designated as
'Negroni Week', a fundraiser
created by *Imbibe Magazine*
where participating bars
donate US$1 to Slow Food
International for each
Negroni served.

NEGRONISKI

INGREDIENTS

60 ml (2 fl oz) vodka

15 ml (½ fl oz) Campari

15 ml (½ fl oz) sweet vermouth

Orange twist, to garnish

METHOD

In a cocktail shaker half-filled with ice, add all the
ingredients, except the garnish, and stir. Strain into
a martini glass and garnish with an orange twist.

DIFFICULTY ★★

NEWPORT NEGRONI

INGREDIENTS

30 ml (1 fl oz) Bombay Sapphire Gin

7 ml (¼ fl oz) Uncle Val's Botanical Gin

20 ml (¾ fl oz) Carpano Antica Formula Vermouth

20 ml (¾ fl oz) Campari

7 ml (¼ fl oz) orange juice

2 dashes of Angostura bitters

METHOD

Add all the ingredients to a cocktail shaker
half-filled with ice, shake, then strain over fresh
ice in a rocks glass.

DIFFICULTY ★★

From Maurice Taylor, Bartending Supervisor,
Brenton Hotel, Newport, Rhode Island, USA

'It's three liquors that I'm not particularly interested in . . . But put them together with a slice of orange. It works . . .'

– Anthony Bourdain

THE OLD PAL

INGREDIENTS

30 ml (1 fl oz) rye whiskey

30 ml (1 fl oz) Dubonnet Rouge

20 ml (¾ fl oz) Lillet Blanc

20 ml (¾ fl oz) Campari

METHOD

Build over ice in a mixing glass and strain into a
rocks glass with a single large ice cube or sphere.

DIFFICULTY ★★

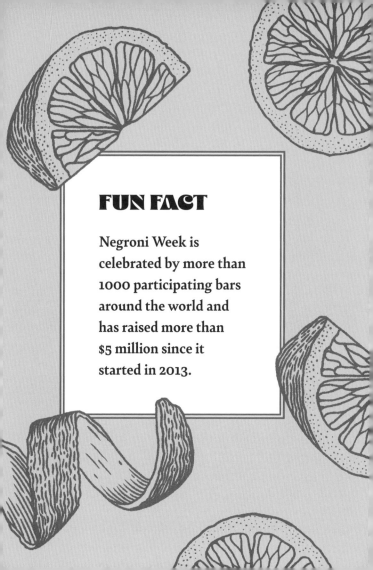

FUN FACT

Negroni Week is celebrated by more than 1000 participating bars around the world and has raised more than $5 million since it started in 2013.

PALMASERA

INGREDIENTS

30 ml (1 fl oz) gin
15 ml (½ fl oz) Campari
15 ml (½ fl oz) blue curaçao
30 ml (1 fl oz) grapefruit juice
Orange twist, to garnish

METHOD

In a cocktail shaker half-filled with ice, add all
the ingredients, except the garnish, and stir. Strain
into a rocks glass over fresh ice. Garnish with an
orange twist.

DIFFICULTY ★★

What's your drink of choice?

'A Negroni Sbagliato (with prosecco in it).'

– Emma D'Arcy

PANTERA ROSA

INGREDIENTS

2 fresh raspberries
15 ml (½ fl oz) light rum
15 ml (½ fl oz) Campari
15 ml (½ fl oz) Cointreau
30 ml (1 fl oz) orange juice
1 small egg white*
Bitter lemon soda
Orange wheel, to garnish

The egg white is meant to give the drink a foamy top. Aquafaba or Fee Foam by Fee Brothers can be substituted.

METHOD

Add all but the soda and garnish to a cocktail shaker half-filled with ice, shake, then strain into a Collins glass over fresh ice. Fill up with bitter lemon soda, stir and garnish with an orange wheel.

DIFFICULTY ★★★

FUN FACT

The world record for the largest Negroni was established in 2022 at the Kimpton Maa-Lai Bangkok Hotel in Thailand. It was 630 litres (139 gallons).

FUN FACT

The most popular food
pairing with Negronis
is pizza.

'That first sip is confusing and not particularly pleasant. But man it grows on you.'

– Anthony Bourdain

PINK TUTU

INGREDIENTS

15 ml (½ fl oz) gin
15 ml (½ fl oz) peach schnapps
15 ml (½ fl oz) Campari
60 ml (2 fl oz) pink grapefruit juice
Orange wheel, to garnish

METHOD

Add all the ingredients, except the garnish, to a
mixing glass half-filled with ice and stir. Strain into
a martini glass and garnish with an orange wheel.

DIFFICULTY ★★

PIRATE'S NEGRONI

INGREDIENTS

30 ml (1 fl oz) black spiced rum (Kraken or Captain Morgan Black)

30 ml (1 fl oz) Campari

30 ml (1 fl oz) sweet vermouth

Maraschino cherry, to garnish

METHOD

Add all the ingredients, except the garnish, to a mixing glass half-filled with ice and stir. Strain into a rocks glass over fresh ice and garnish with a maraschino cherry on a cocktail skewer.

DIFFICULTY ★★

RAFFINO

INGREDIENTS

30 ml (1 fl oz) dry vermouth

15 ml (½ fl oz) Campari

15 ml (½ fl oz) gin

15 ml (½ fl oz) lime juice

Lime wheel, to garnish

METHOD

Add all the ingredients, except the garnish, to a
mixing glass half-filled with ice and stir. Strain
into a rocks glass over fresh ice and garnish with
a lime wheel.

DIFFICULTY ★★

SHERRY'S NEGRONI

INGREDIENTS

45 ml (1½ fl oz) dry sherry
30 ml (1 fl oz) sweet vermouth
20 ml (¾ fl oz) Campari
Orange wheel, to garnish

METHOD

Add all the ingredients, except the garnish, to a
mixing glass half-filled with ice and stir. Strain
into a rocks glass over fresh ice and garnish with an
orange wheel.

DIFFICULTY ★★

SOPRANO

INGREDIENTS

60 ml (2 fl oz) whiskey

30 ml (1 fl oz) amaretto

15 ml (½ fl oz) simple syrup

7 ml (¼ fl oz) Campari

Orange wheel, to garnish

METHOD

Add all the ingredients, except the garnish, to a cocktail shaker half-filled with ice. Shake and strain into a martini glass. Garnish with an orange wheel.

DIFFICULTY ★★

'For me,
the Negroni
will always
be the
drink of
initiation
and
liberation.'

– Graham Swift

STRAWBERRY BLONDE NEGRONI

INGREDIENTS

60 ml (2 fl oz) strawberry vodka

15 ml (½ fl oz) Campari

15 ml (½ fl oz) dry vermouth

Sliced strawberry, to garnish

METHOD

Add all the ingredients, except the garnish, to a cocktail shaker half-filled with ice. Shake and strain into a martini glass. Garnish with a sliced strawberry.

DIFFICULTY ★★

TESTAROSSA

INGREDIENTS

30 ml (1 fl oz) vodka
30 ml (1 fl oz) Campari
30 ml (1 fl oz) club soda
Orange twist, to garnish

METHOD

Add the vodka and Campari to a cocktail shaker half-filled with ice. Shake and strain into a rocks glass filled with fresh ice and top up with club soda. Garnish with an orange twist.

DIFFICULTY ★★

'Naturally, I'm misanthropic. But the Negronis are helping considerably.'

– Anthony Bourdain

VENETIAN SUNSET

INGREDIENTS

45 ml (1½ fl oz) gin

20 ml (¾ fl oz) dry vermouth

20 ml (¾ fl oz) orange curaçao

20 ml (¾ fl oz) Campari

Orange twist or wheel, to garnish

METHOD

Add all the ingredients, except the garnish, to a cocktail shaker half-filled with ice. Shake and strain into a rocks glass filled with fresh ice. Garnish with an orange twist or orange wheel.

DIFFICULTY ★★

FUN FACT

Ernest Hemingway
liked Negronis so much
that he named one of
his dogs Negroni.

FUN FACT

Audrey Hepburn served
Negronis at her Rome
house parties while
filming *Roman Holiday*.

WHITE NEGRONI

INGREDIENTS

45 ml (1½ fl oz) gin
20 ml (¾ fl oz) Suze*
20 ml (¾ fl oz) vermouth bianco
Lemon twist, to garnish

Suze is a bitter French aperitif imported by Pernod Ricard.

METHOD

Add all the ingredients, except the garnish, to a cocktail shaker half-filled with ice. Stir and strain into a rocks glass filled with fresh ice. Garnish with a lemon twist.

DIFFICULTY ★★

Adapted from Nick Blacknell, 2001

'Perfect drink on a hangover.'

– Alex Payne,
The Rectory Hotel, Cotswolds, UK

WHITE NEGRONI SOUR

INGREDIENTS

20 ml (¾ fl oz) gin
20 ml (¾ fl oz) Campari
20 ml (¾ fl oz) dry vermouth
15 ml (½ fl oz) grapefruit juice
15 ml (½ fl oz) lime juice
Dash of orange bitters
1 small egg white*
Orange twist, to garnish

The egg white is meant to give the drink a foamy top. Aquafaba or Fee Foam by Fee Brothers can be substituted.

METHOD

Add all the ingredients, except the garnish, to a cocktail shaker half-filled with ice. Shake vigorously and strain into a rocks glass filled with fresh ice. Garnish with an orange twist.

DIFFICULTY ★★★